Mariam ♡

I got myself a copy too.
I thought of you when I bought
this. Hope we can share
our fav pieces to one
another!

♡ Aaron

BOOKS BY GUILLAUME WOLF "PROF. G"

- *You Are a Quest*
- *You Are a Dream*
- *You Are a Message*
- *You Are a Circle*
- *Super Hyper Vibe!*

For information about the author, online creative workshops, and additional content, please visit **www.ProfG.co**

YOU ARE A QUEST

A VISUAL MEDITATION FOR THE CREATIVE SOUL

GUILLAUME WOLF "PROF. G"

SECOND EDITION

Texts and art: Guillaume Wolf.
Copy editor: Kristin M. Jones.

Web content. *You Are a Quest* comes with additional online content. This limited, complimentary offer is open to all purchasers of *You Are a Quest*—to access the Web content, you must have a valid e-mail address. This offer is limited: Content and registration is subject to availability or change. By providing your e-mail address, you give the author permission to send you information on products, news, and services. In order to protect your privacy, the author does not sell, share, or trade the subscriber list with anyone for any reason. E-mail is never sent unsolicited and is only delivered to users who have provided their e-mail address in agreement to receive these e-mails. You may unsubscribe at any time. Although the offer is complimentary, the participants will be responsible for the electronic equipment needed to access the content. Neither the publisher nor the author shall be liable for any loss of profit or other commercial damages, including but not limited to special, incidental, consequential, or other damages. The terms of this offer can be changed at any time.

For Margaux and Joanne,

with all my love.

For Miguel,

in creative friendship.

THIS IS NOT REALLY A BOOK.

This an experience, a visual meditation about life, creativity, love, and the human spirit. **This is just for you, my creative friend.** This is is a moment of peace, inspiration, and introspection.

You can look at the geometric shapes and let them speak to you, or you can read the little aphorisms and ponder them. Start from the beginning, the middle, or the end—do whatever you want. This is your moment.

You Are a Quest is an invitation to look at your life as an adventure—a call to explore, create, love, and shine. Not someday in the future, but *right now*. As you're reading these words, take a break and look around you. What do you see? **Are you ready to make your reality as extraordinary as you'd like it to be?**

Be very mindful—the quest is real. **Your life is calling you,** at this very moment, to start your journey.

Now is the time to answer the call.

Shine on, little star. Shine on.
Let your light out.

With love,
Guillaume Wolf "Prof. G"

EXPLORE

The quest is invisible,
But it wants to show you a new reality.
The quest is quiet,
But it's screaming your name.
The quest is still,
But it wants you to act.
The quest offers no promises,
But it demands your commitment.

The quest is your journey
Into the unknown
To find yourself.
Are *you* ready for it?

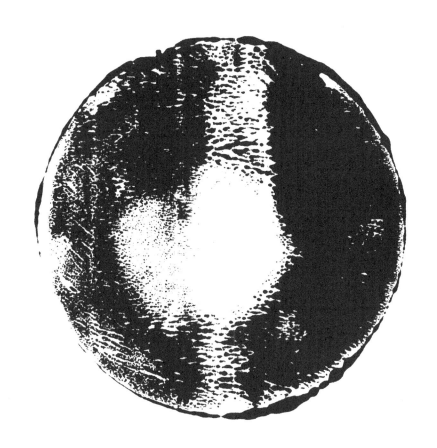

Your great adventure isn't something
That will happen to you someday.
It's here already.
Your great adventure is happening right now.

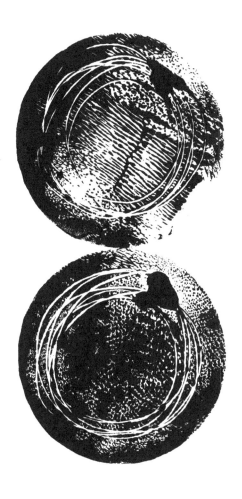

You're a drop of rain,
Born out of a cloud,
Falling into the ocean.

Are you separated?
Are you one?

Are you time-bound?
Are you infinite?

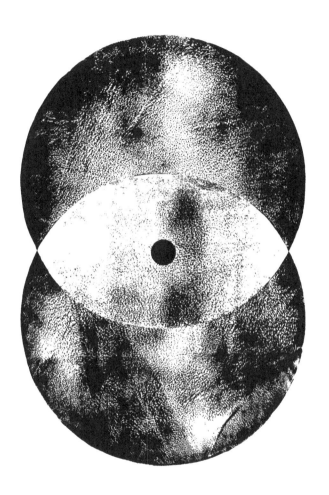

Explore something new,
Something exciting.
Just because.
Lose yourself in the experience
Of this magic moment.

If you're alive today,
You're rich in time.
You're rich in life.

Feel it deeply
Until you really get it.

Here's a secret:
Your beliefs about yourself, life,
Situations, and people
Define your reality.

And everywhere you go,
Your experience of reality
Confirms your beliefs.

This is the perfect trap.

But the day you start
Questioning these beliefs,
And move beyond them,
Something magical happens:
The whole world unfolds.

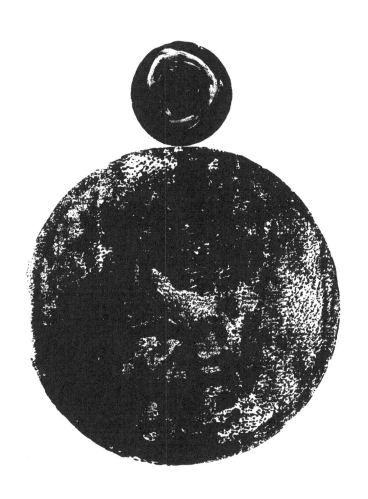

Humanity loves stories of unlikely heroes,
Wizards, monsters, epic battles, and hidden treasures.
We have told these stories since the dawn of time.

Why?

Because we are all unlikely heroes.
We must learn about the magic of life.
We must conquer our darkest thoughts.
We must fight against incredible odds
To find the hidden treasures.

The quest is real.
It lives within.

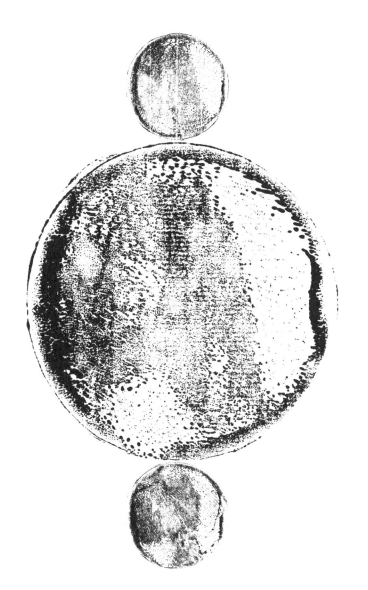

Be curious.
Try new things.
Right now!
There are so many possibilities.
Decide!

Everything good in your life today
Comes from tiny decisions
You've made in the past.

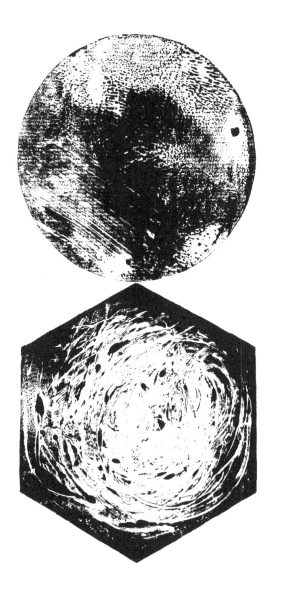

Your life, as it is today,
Is your opportunity to grow, love,
Create, and play.
Own it.

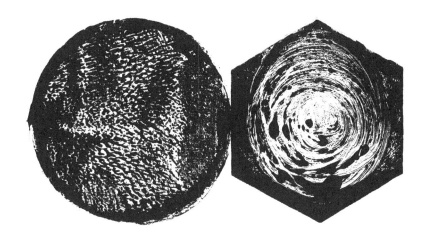

How can I express myself?
How can I experience life to the fullest?
How can I bring love into the present?

Every day, answer these questions.
This is the way of mastery.

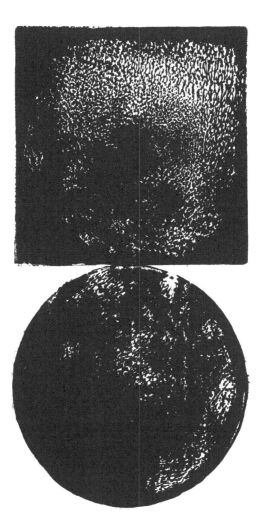

Life is a mystery.
When you decide to bring awareness
To every little moment,
When you stay present,
Life starts speaking to you.

Your time is now.
Make it count.
You're worth your time.

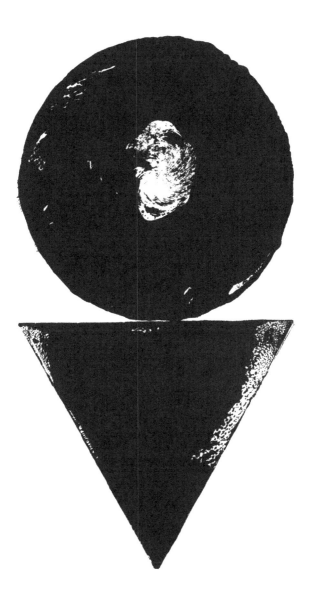

The change you want outside
Begins with change inside.
Do you want change?
Change!

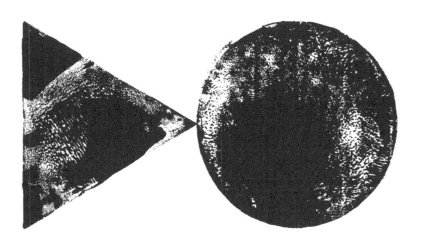

Pick up a pencil, a guitar, or some clay.
Let's see what your hands can do.
Get a camera and go outside.
What will your eyes discover?
Go to the market and get some fresh produce.
What new taste will you explore?
Put some music on and start to dance.
Can you disappear into movement?
It really doesn't matter
How you choose to express yourself.
What's important is to let out
What's inside of you.

If I were you, I would
Be amazed to see
All the things I could do.
If I were you, I would
Be excited to explore even more.
If I were you, I would
Never give up.
If I were you, I would
Stop trying to be perfect.
If I were you, I would
Speak my truth, love, and create.

Why?

Because I see through you.
I see all your untapped potential.
I see your beauty and your strength.
I see your uniqueness.

Now, if YOU were YOU,
What would *YOU* do?

Your greatest chance
Is recognizing that, today,
There are infinite ways to live,
Work, love, and be happy.

Your greatest obstacle
Is giving up on exploring
What these possibilities could
Actually mean for you.

If surrendering to the power of a new experience
Is an idea that scares you,
Then your need for control is controlling you.
Get this:
Freedom comes from experiencing the possibilities of the new.
You must always choose transformation over stagnation.
That's the only way to be alive.

At a primal level,
Reality is experienced through energy.
Everything you think, say, or do
Has a unique energy signature.
Be aware of it.
Expand it.
Play with it.
Project it.

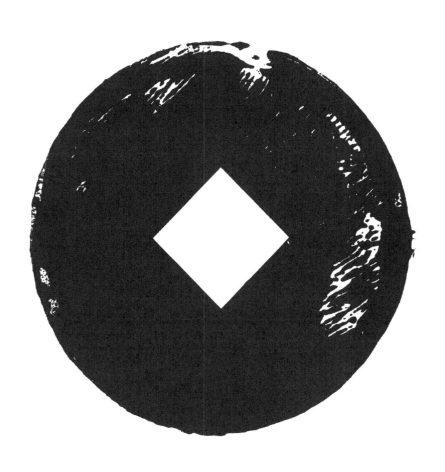

No matter who you are,
No matter what you do,
Ask yourself:
How can I create a unique experience?
And once you do,
Life will surprise you.

Your oversoul overstands
The well-lived moment.
What's your next move?

Everything is possible
When you push beyond
What you think is possible.

Everything is possible
When you feel beyond
What you believe is possible.

All of your gestures
Are resonating with the cosmos.

You are a living power
Connected with everything.

When you create,
The universe sings with you.

The meaning you're seeking in your life
Will not come through buying things you don't need.
It will come through unfolding your True Self into the world.
How?
Start by listening to your heart.
Pay attention.
Do you hear what it says?

Micro meditation challenge.
Do it for a week:

Every time you wash your hands,
Make a big soap bubble.
Look at it deeply.
See beauty.
See perfection.
Until it pops.

There's hidden power
In this simple practice.
The little things can tell you stories
About everything.

Be unreasonable.
Dream about something impossible.
Think about something impossible.
Try something impossible.
Try again.
Try again.
Try again.
Look!
You have made the impossible real!

If one moment
Contains all of time,

If one situation
Contains everything there is,

There are no limits
To what you can imagine, create,
And experience.

Don't try to find answers in everything.
The mystery of your life
Is bigger than you think it is.

Instead, accept the unknown,
And feel the thrill of being alive
By being one with this moment.

Imagine having a bag of seeds,
But refusing to plant and water them.
That's the trap of overthinking everything.
Ongoing action gives you something
That thinking alone cannot: the feedback of reality.
That's where real learning comes from.

Make a choice and act on it.
Act a lot and you'll see your garden grow.

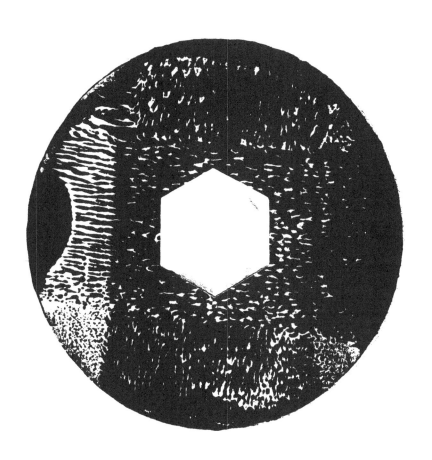

ON

EXPLORING

Guillaume Wolf "Prof. G" talks with Joanne Abellera about some of the ideas presented in *You Are a Quest*.

Fiber artist and fashion designer Joanne Abellera is Guillaume Wolf's life partner. Together, they live and work in their mountain home in Lake Arrowhead, California, with their daughter.

Joanne Abellera: *So, let's start with the quest. What is it about?*

Guillaume Wolf: The quest is the quest to find yourself. It's the adventure hidden inside your own life . . . waiting for you to activate it.

JA: *How do you do that?*

GW: It starts in your own mind, by thinking new thoughts, by allowing yourself to dream bigger. Then, going outside of your comfort zone and starting something new.

JA: *Can you give some examples?*

GW: Sure, traveling to a foreign country—getting to know a new culture—could be the beginning of the journey. It can also start with a new activity. For example, let's say you begin by exploring photography. You get a camera, and you commit to publishing a little zine three times a year. It could also be starting a new business. Any creative project you can think about will do.

JA: *How so?*

GW: It's about this idea of the encounter with life, your willingness to meet with a new situation and bring your full presence to whatever might come up. Allowing the unknown into your life . . . that's how you can find yourself.

JA: *Can you explain this idea of "finding yourself"? If I know who I am, did I not find myself already?*

GW: This is the core question at the heart of everything: "Do you really know who you are?" And by that, I mean, do you know your True Self, beyond your surface-level conditioned self (that I call the Persona). This is a very powerful question.

JA: *Because we don't even know about it?*

GW: Exactly. We are born into a country, a society, a culture, a family unit. And as a result, growing up, we take on a conditioned self that thinks for us. And we don't question it. So, most of the time, we live automatically. And the problem is that this Persona doesn't really do a great job at ruling our lives. At some point, we might hit a wall. We wake up and we feel miserable. And for many people, there's this moment of crisis, where we start asking ourselves: "Why is my life not working the way I want it to?" This is "the dark night of the soul." And this crisis *is* the call. This is where the quest can begin.

JA: *The quest is about personal growth?*

GW: Yes, but in a radical way. It's about a transformation. To unfold into your True Self, you need to let your old self go. That's what it's about. This is not easy.

JA: *You write: "Never wish for a different life."*

GW: Yes, and this is extremely important: Everyone's quest is unique. And your quest is available to you, right now, no matter who you are. If you look at your life, at this very moment, and think, "This is so boring!" This is where your adventure begins. If you look and say, "There's so much pain or anger," again, this is where it begins for you. It doesn't matter where you come from, your life contains this adventure about growth and exploration—this unique possibility. Your life can be "a journey into power," "a journey into love," or "a journey into healing or peace" . . . but it's your job to activate it.

JA: *In the quotes, you say: "You're worth your time."*

GW: Of course you are! The gem is within your own life. You're worth exploring what this could mean for you. Your quest is your big adventure.

JA: *You also write: "Your greatest chance is recognizing that, today, there are infinite ways to live, work, love, and be happy."*

GW: Yes, this is key, and exploring these possibilities is really what your life should be about. Not living life by default, or living someone else's dream, but living by inspiration. And here— I want to be clear—this takes courage. You have to be your own champion; no one will do it for you. But the potential is here.

JA: *One of the most poetic and mysterious quotes from this section goes like this: "You're a drop of rain, born out of a cloud, falling into the ocean." Can you explain it a little bit?*

GW: This is a way to talk about human existence—which fascinates me. And this metaphor of the drop of rain is something that I love using because it works so well. We appear into human life out of a great void. Our existence is really short. Then, we return into the great void. So it seems we're in between two states. But if you think about the drop of rain, you see that even though it seems to be differentiated from the cloud and the ocean, it's also one and the same. I think it's very healthy to see our existence this way—integrated, and a part of a bigger whole. Because if we are one, there's no reason to live in fear.

JA: *In your own life, have you applied these principles? What did you get from them?*

GW: Yes, of course. Throughout my life, I've applied these ideas. First, I've explored what was possible by really pushing myself outside of my comfort zone. This allowed me to expand personally and professionally. And while I grew up in Paris, I now live in California—a completely different life and culture. It's really amazing to have created this possibility. But on the inside, I feel it's even more rewarding. It's like a never-ending gift where you can ask yourself: "Where can I grow now?" And you go and do it. This is where the magic is for me.

CREATE

Go create.
The more you create, the more you grow.
The more you grow, the more change happens.
Stop wondering, start creating.

Create and tell me a story.
Remind me that humanity
Is worth something good.
Make me believe in possibilities.
That's the key.

Dreaming with certainty.
Creating the life you want.
It's not about luck.
It's about using your creative energy
To grow into the best person you can be.
Become great by acting great,
And you'll manifest greatness.

To become a master creator,
Cultivate the beginner's mind.
"Know that you don't know."
Enter your creative process
With the sole goal of exploring something new.
This opens up endless possibilities.

Today, place yourself in an active state of receptivity.
What's happening in your life?
What's going on in the lives of others?
What's going on in the world?
Pay attention: There is an idea—right in front of you.
You have all the elements.
Open your eyes! Be present!
Your life is a game asking you to connect the dots.

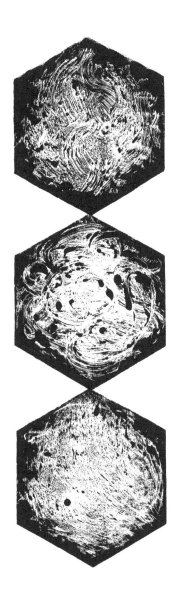

Want less.
Create more.

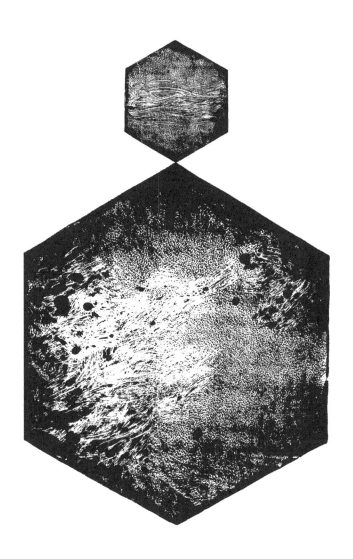

It's not about what you did before,
Your past successes, or your failures.
It's what you're doing *today*.

To create, you must stand in the present
Because nothing else truly exists.
You only exist in the present.

No one can ever give you permission to create.
The real magic is already within you.
It's your job to let it out.

Life wants to know:
Are you in reaction?
Or
Are you in creation?

There's a magic power . . .
It's called patience.
When you start focusing on goals
That might take ten years to achieve,
And every single day you take a stab at them,
You become an unstoppable force.

Patience teaches you
To love the process,
Which is the most important
Lesson you'll ever need.

Patience is rarer than gold.
Find it within you,
And you'll become a master of life.

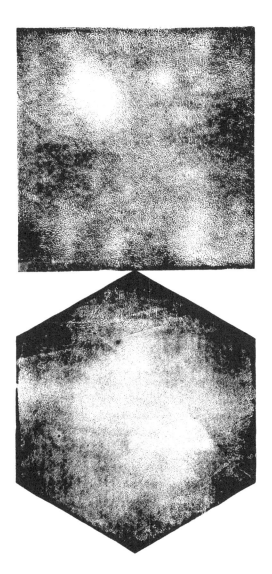

If you feel lonely as a creator,
Learn to connect with others.

Creating your work is not enough.
You need to release it into the world.

You must create *and* connect.

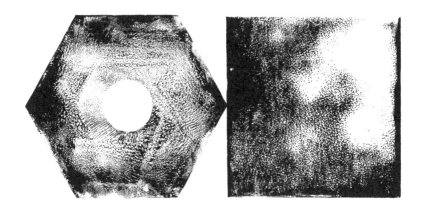

At the highest level, a creator is someone
Who has the capacity to create a new reality.

At the lowest level, it's someone
Who always feels trapped by her reality.

Good or bad, we're all creators.

The difference is awareness.
Recognizing that you're always creating,
And being willing to jump in and do the work.
This will bring the change you desire.

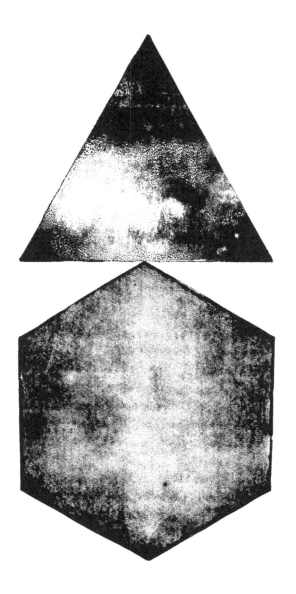

Be a creative leader.
Lead yourself.
Say what you want to do.
Do what you want to say.

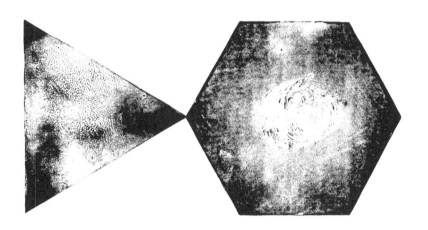

You are a great storyteller.
You tell stories about your past.
You tell stories about your present.
You tell stories about your future.

You are a great actor.
You always act the part perfectly,
Following your storyline.

Are your stories serving you?
What new stories would you like to create
And be a part of?
These are great questions.

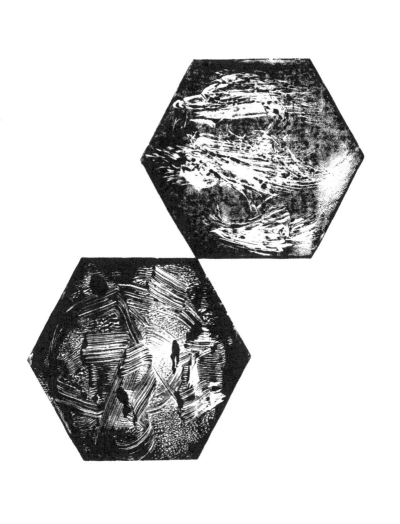

The creative essence is the foundation of nature.
Its sequence: ideation, growth, multiplication, dissolution.
The creative essence is the foundation of who you are.
Learn how you can bring its sequence
Into every aspect of your life.

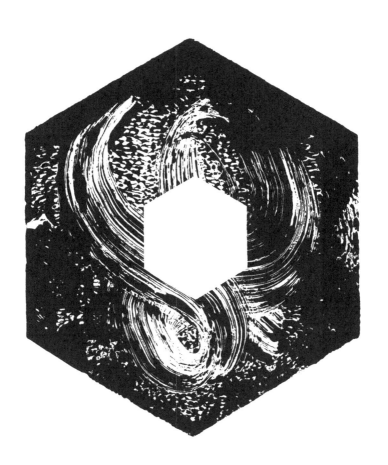

Don't follow trends.
Create a new path.
Do the opposite of what
The herd is doing.

Look at nature:
Dripping water can pierce a hole through a rock.
Look at yourself:
Creative effort can alter the fabric of your reality.

Too much leisure is tiring.
Too much food is sickening.
Too much ecstasy is painful.

Unlimited pleasure is a path
That cannot bring long-term rewards.

Now, why do you think
Creative life is so hard?

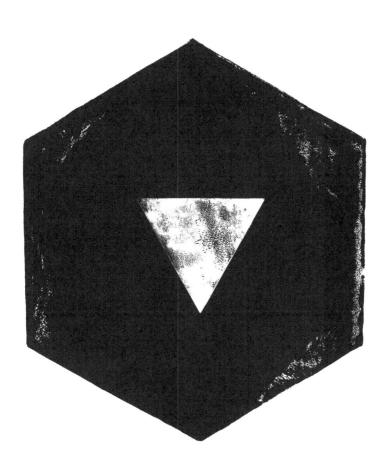

Your natural potential is creativity.
How can you express it into the world?
Just start.
It can be anything.
It's not what you do,
It's the fact that you're doing it.

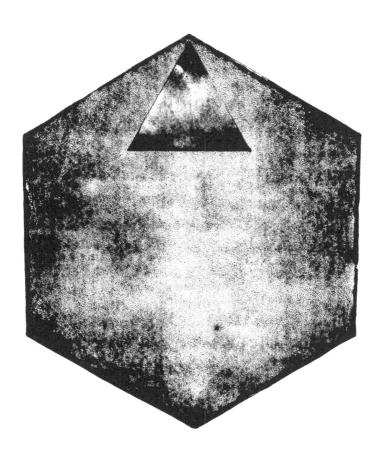

Watch out:
Your comfort zone
Is a hypnotic monster,
Sucking the life out of you.
Quick!
Do something uncomfortable!
This is the only way to grow.

Information
Space
Time
Energy
Matter

These are the five elements
Of the creative magician.

What you fear can make you stronger
If you bring it into your creative work.
Creativity is alchemy.

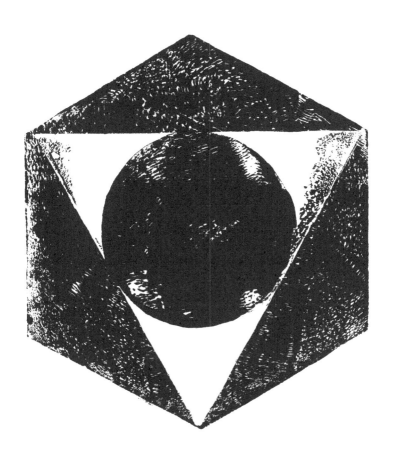

There's an infinity of thoughts in humanity.
There's infinity of dreams in your mind.
When you create,
You bring a little bit of infinity into the world
For all of us to see and experience.

To become a tree, let go of being an acorn.
To become a creator, let go of your old self.

You are constantly changing.
A creative mutant.
Transformation is your game.
And if you play it well,
Transcendence is your reward.

Up and down.
Hot and cold.
Bright and dark.
Old and new.
Small and big.
Opposites create new patterns
That alter reality.

To jump ahead,
Play with opposites.
Create a new pattern.

Creativity and equanimity.
If you can bring both into your life,
You will have found the ultimate treasure.

We've never met,
But I hope one day we will,
So you can tell me what you've created
And the beauty that blossomed.

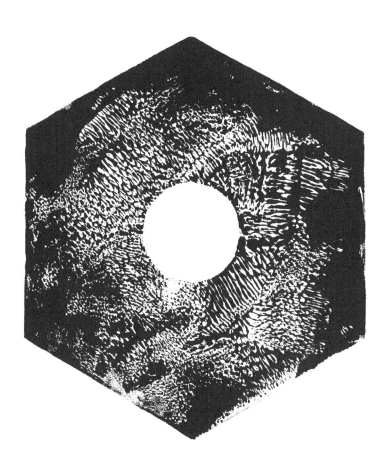

ON

CREATING

Joanne Abellera: *As a teacher, you teach creative skills. What's the most important one?*

Guillaume Wolf: It's allowing yourself to experiment. Doing something just to see what might come up—without knowing the outcome (instead of wanting to get a result in advance). Being open—that's how you end up creating the new.

JA: *You talk about the beginner's mind.*

GW: Yes, I wrote "Know that you don't know." This is a state of mind. This is how you can stay open to the possibilities of the present moment. This is how you're able to keep on trying, because it's part of your process.

JA: *How important is creativity today?*

GW: I would say that it has become a vital skill for everyone. Today, the world is changing so fast, an entire industry can disappear overnight. So, from the perspective of the individual, it's very important to be adaptive. Creativity allows you to do that because it's the habit of creating new possibilities for yourself.

JA: *A lot of people want to create something new but they are paralyzed by fear.*

GW: Yes, this is the norm.

JA: *How do you move beyond fear?*

GW: This calls for a deeper conversation, and I talk about it in my previous book (*You Are a Dream*). The key I want to share here is that you can't overthink your fears. So thinking about it will do you no good. You have to act. So, in a sense, creativity is about coming into your own power. You have to start something new, and treat it like an experiment. See how it goes.

Get some feedback and adjust your approach. It's a process of ongoing refinement through action.

JA: *But what if you can't act because of the fear?*

GW: You have to be super clear on what fear is. First, at the highest level, life is change. That's a fundamental principle. In total opposite, you have fear. Fear lies to you and makes you believe that, in order to be safe, stagnating—or staying the same—is the right thing to do. This is an awful lie! Stagnation is death. Everything and everyone that's alive (what I call a living system) is here to expand and grow. Once you really get this at the core of your being, creative expansion is the only way to go. Expansion *is* life.

JA: *You also talk about patience. You say "It's rarer than gold."*

GW: Yes! [*laughs*] Because, you see, you have to get that your creative gesture is an ongoing process—it never stops. And you have to love your process. So patience is key. To put it differently, your life is like a never-ending puzzle that keeps evolving. Life is here to teach you patience.

JA: *You also add, "Good or bad, we're all creators."*

GW: Yes, we are co-creating reality. We're all doing it, whether we're aware of it or not. First, you have objective reality (a situation that occurs), and then there's subjective reality, how you interpret it . . . the meaning you give to it. This interpretation—or this translation of reality—is always an act of creation. And you have to watch out . . . You have to be very careful with it.

JA: *Can you give an example?*

GW: Well, let's imagine that you live in a nice house with your partner, you have a lovely family. A dog. Two cars. Anybody from the outside who looks at your life objectively would say: "She has a nice life."

JA: *Sure.*

GW: But hold on . . . because in our story, you spend all your time on social media, comparing your life to others, and here's what you see, big mansions, exotic cars, amazing vacations. And now, you look at your life and you feel awful. You hate your life because you've created an interpretation that says: "It's not good enough."

JA: *That's the disease of our times, right?*

GW: Yes, and here, I want to say that there are no limits on how miserable you can make yourself. It has nothing to do with how much you have. I know millionaires who always feel that they're not good enough. So it's not about that. It's how you're creating reality. How you perceive reality is always an act of creation. It's a subjective process. You're always fabricating stories about everything around you, thinking it's the truth. You have to be very careful. This is why I'm asking: "Are your stories serving you?" This is a powerful question.

JA: *When you change your stories, you change your life?*

GW: Yes. But first, you need to be aware that you're doing these translations of reality—and question them. You need to recognize that these interpretations are shaping your experience of what actually is. Once you're clear on this, you can start creating new stories—and acting—in a way that empowers you.

JA: *You also write: "To create, you must stand in the present . . . because nothing else truly exists."*

GW: Yes, then I add, "You only exist in the present." This is an important idea. We've been talking about these stories we're all creating . . . these interpretations. Well, . . . you're doing it to yourself, and others are doing it to you. All your life, you've been surrounded by stories that are pressuring you—by telling you what's possible and what's not possible.

In total contrast, when you make the effort to disregard all these stories; now, you can step into the present. It's like being reborn into what *is*. For the first time, you can be here, now—as you are. You can connect with what's possible at this very moment. When you do this, you'll find that there are many directions you can take. There are many ways you can grow. There are many things you can learn or experience.

From this place, your first act of creation can completely change your destiny. This is the key to freedom.

LOVE

When you love,
Life is infinite.

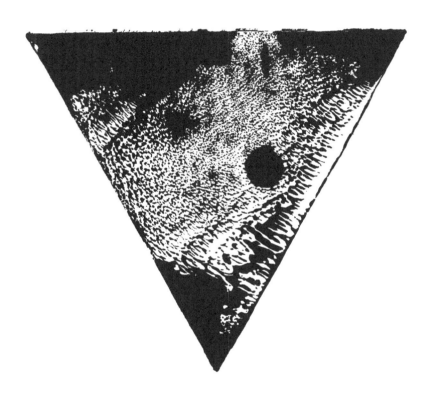

Love is a power
That power can't tame.
Feel this mighty love.
Feel it now.

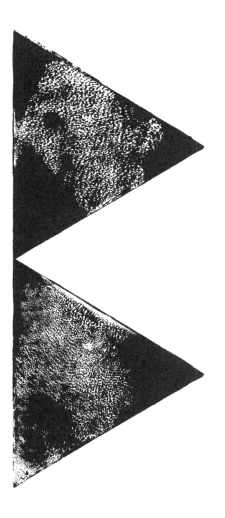

Awaken into life.
Awaken into love.

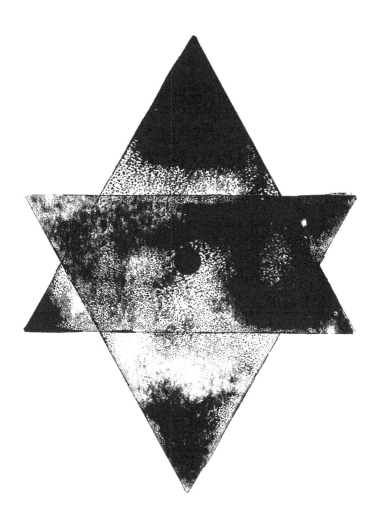

You are a unique individual.
You are filled with possibilities,
Gifts, and desires
That want to be expressed
Into the world.
This is beautiful.
You are beautiful.

Life is short,
Love is big.
Love yourself,
Love others,
Love life.

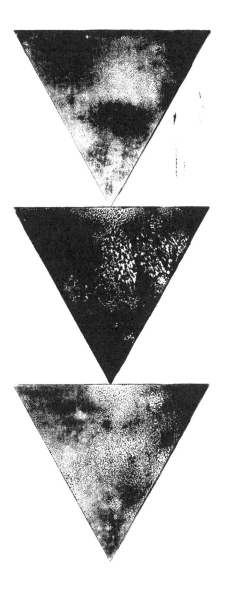

Remember:
You're lovable and capable.
Remember?
You're lovable and capable.
Always remember.

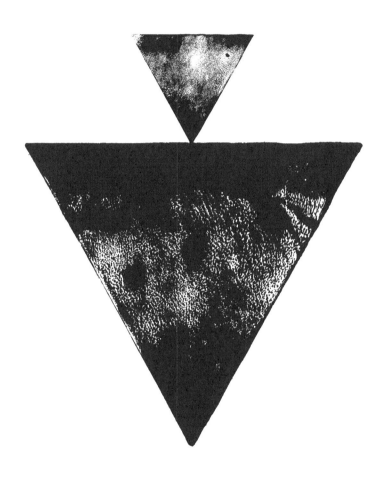

Life is about
Being,
Doing,
Playing,
Loving.
Right here.
Right now.

If you open your heart,
You'll discover that
The love you seek
Is already there.

You're one
With the beloved,
Within and without.

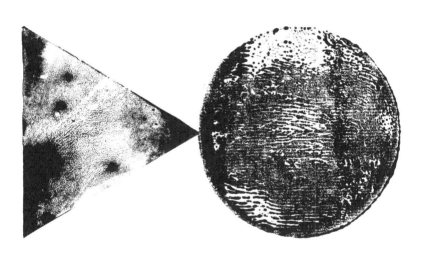

Don't confuse love with desire.
Don't confuse experience with possession.
Don't confuse presence with control.

Wanting is not the same as being.

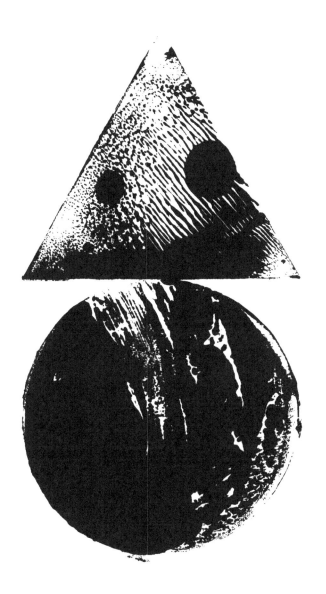

Be gentle.

You don't need to put so much pressure
On yourself.

Let life bring the pressure.
You take care of bringing the love.

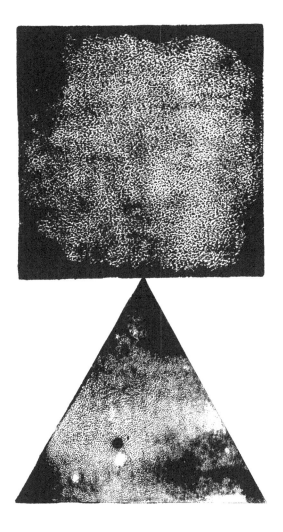

Love isn't just a noun.
It's a verb.
Use it often.

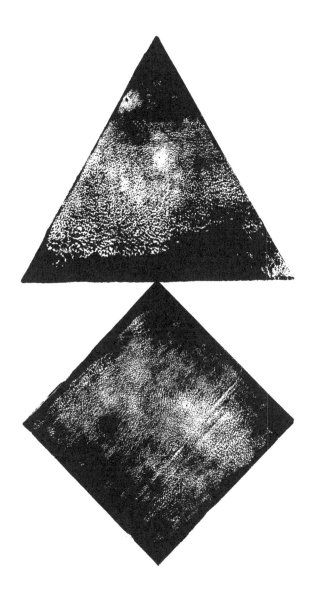

True love is being here.
Being in love with the gift of life.

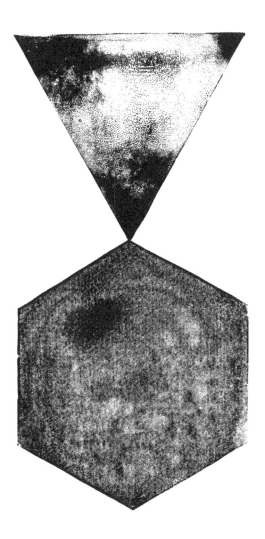

Extreme suffering.
Extreme beauty.
Love behind it all . . .
What a show this life is!

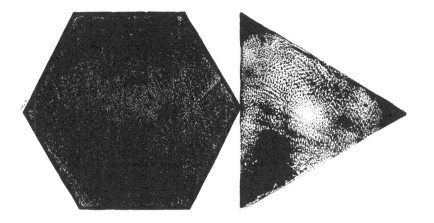

Real love goes beyond time.
If you've lost a loved one,
A presence might be missing,
But your love will always remain.
This connection can never be broken.

Love without contingency is freedom.
Love without boundaries is higher wisdom.

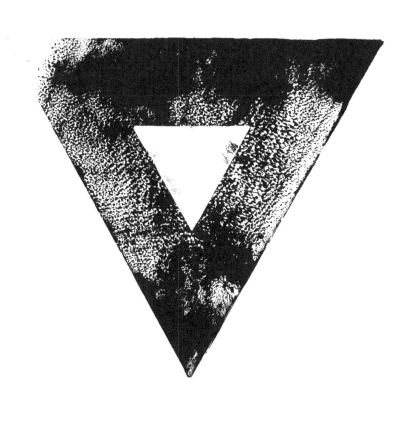

Bring love
Doing the dishes,
Taking out the trash,
And cleaning the house.
You will live well.

When you have love,
The world is dancing with you.
Wait—look!
You have love!

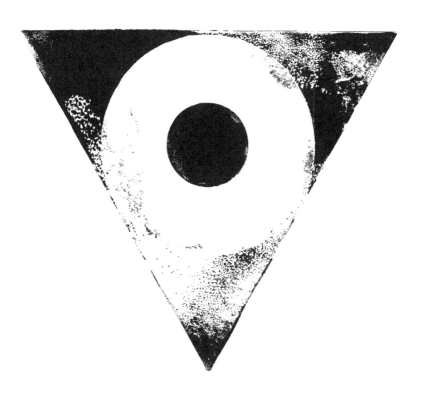

If you try to contain love,
And put it in a box,
It turns into pain.
Love is meant to move freely,
In and out of existence.
Transcend your need to grasp.
If you allow love to flow,
It will never go away.

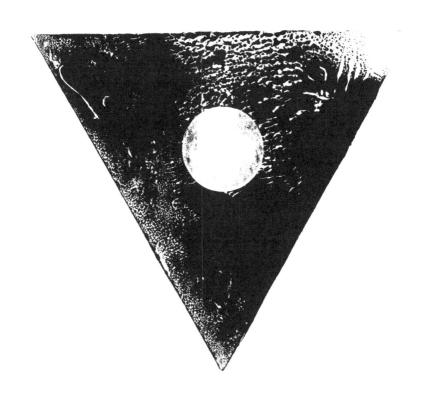

Life is waiting for you
To fall in love with life,
So life can fall in love with you.

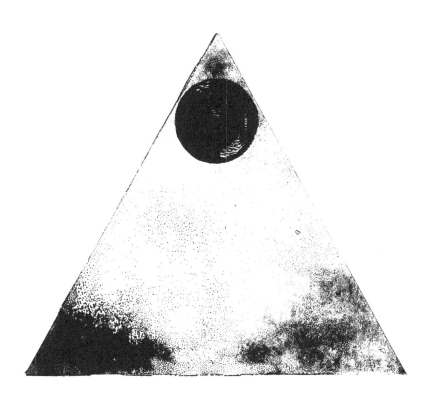

Love the process
Of discovering
What your life
Is all about.

Find the gem
That's hidden.

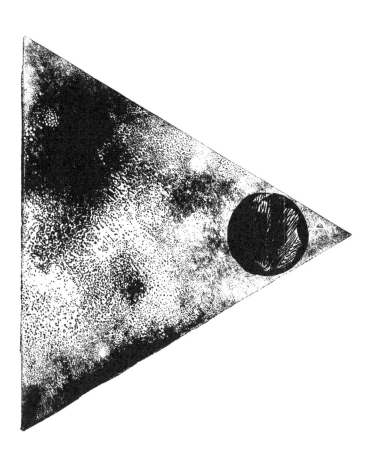

Love is unlimited energy.
Bring love into your life
To create more love.

Gratitude is the way to love.
Look around,
Search for what's beautiful, meaningful,
And true in your life.
Open your heart to the little things
That you take for granted.

When you bless the present with gratitude,
The present blesses you with love.

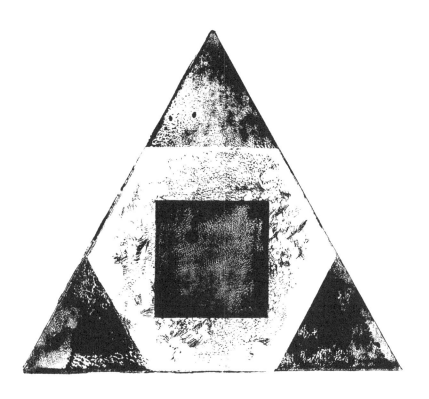

Feeling unloved?
Start loving yourself first.
That's right.
Love everything about yourself:
The good, the bad, and the crazy.
Love yourself deep and wide.
Love yourself by learning, by growing,
By exploring, by expressing yourself.
Love yourself by saying, No!
Love yourself by saying, Yes!
Love your courage, your wit, and your curiosity.
Love your imperfections.
Love it all.
Because once you start loving yourself,
You become a radiant sun.

I see you.
You are full of love.
I see you.
Do you see yourself?

Love is magic.
Magic is love.
You are magic.
I love you.

Be present for what *is*.
Look deeply.
Cherish what's here already.

Even if you did not grow up with love in your life,
Know that you can create a life full of love.
Just bring it.
Love unfolds into love.

The math of love is weird.
1 + 1 = 3
Your act of love multiplies reality.

ON

LOVING

Joanne Abellera: *Your opening quote on love is "When you love, life is infinite." Can you expand on that?*

Guillaume Wolf: Yes, but first I'd like to define what I mean by "love," because I think there's a lot of confusion on the subject in our society.

JA: *Yes.*

GW: Many people are confusing love with possession or desire. Meaning, when they say, "I love you," what they really say is, "I want you to be mine in the way I want you to be." This is extremely common. Someone falls in love with an image—an image that he/she has created. And later, once this creation turns out to be an actual person, there's a feeling of betrayal: "Why can't you be more like the way I've imagined you!" [*laughs*]

JA: *They project an image onto someone.*

GW: Yes; so here, we're not talking about that.

JA: *So what kind of love are you talking about?*

GW: I'm talking about the love that comes from presence. If I give my full presence to someone, myself, or a situation, love comes in. Unconditional love.

JA: *So when there's no clutter, love arises?*

GW: Yes, you can say that.

JA: *Let's go back to my question: "When you love, life is infinite," what is it about?*

GW: This is about the nature of love. You see, love is unlike any other energy. It's unlimited. Love is infinite. And yes, when you love, life becomes infinite because love colors everything it touches.

JA: *But this is hard to get. Let's imagine that you love someone, but they pass away.*

GW: They can live forever in your heart. Unfolding this infinite love is something *you* do.

JA: *You write: "The love you seek is already there. You're one with the beloved, within and without."*

GW: Yes, going back to romantic love, there's also this idea that, one day, you will find someone to make you whole—a soulmate. And having a soulmate is great . . . but it's not his/her job to make you whole!

JA: *That would be too much pressure!*

GW: And so this search for wholeness is not something that you will find outside of you. This love that you seek, you must find it first within yourself. The love is there. And here, what I'm talking about is transcendent love. Because love, at the highest level, connects us to the infinite. A love that's bigger than everything. A love that transcends everything.

JA: *Everything?*

GW: Yes. This goes back to discovering what's the fabric of reality. Some theoretical physicists offer that the core of matter is information. But information is never neutral, isn't it? And here, if you decide to look at reality and say, "At the very core, the fundamental is love," this is the ultimate shift in perspective. Ultimate love in all. This opens the door to finding the sacred in your heart . . . because if love permeates all, then *you* are love.

JA: *Does it mean we're interconnected?*

GW: Yes, it means that we are one. I am you and you are me. Everything is one. Love is all.

JA: *But what if you did not grow up with love?*

GW: This is important that we talk about this. If you've never received love, you can always bring it back into your life. No one can take that away from you. At first it might feel a bit awkward, and that's fine. But the more you put love into your reality, the more you will experience it. Start infusing your reality with love. Give love a chance . . . See what happens . . .

JA: *One of my favorite quotes in this section is "Life is waiting for you to fall in love with life."*

GW: Yes, there's this living relationship between you and life, and the thread is love. If you bring it into life, life will bring it back to you.

JA: *How does gratitude play into this relationship?*

GW: As a daily practice, gratitude is a wonderful path to love. I think everyone should have a gratitude journal. It's really simple: At the end of each day, you write what you're grateful for, the little things. That's all there is to it. It pacifies your mind by offering a perspective based on love. It's really an incredible, transformative practice.

SHINE

Be curious to discover what you can really do.
Act beyond your imaginary limitations:
You'll surprise yourself.

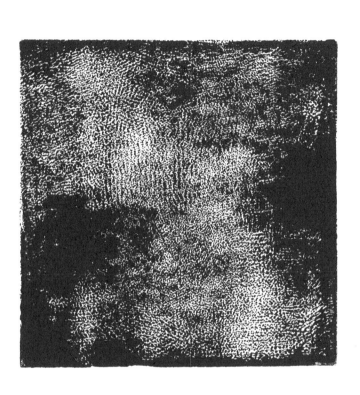

Feel you have no time?
Take a deep breath:
Focus on your breathing.
Connect with your core.
You'll uncover the timeless
In no time.

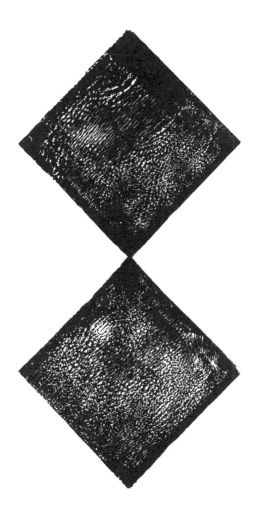

You don't play a game because you have to.
You play because you want to.
How are you playing the game of your life?

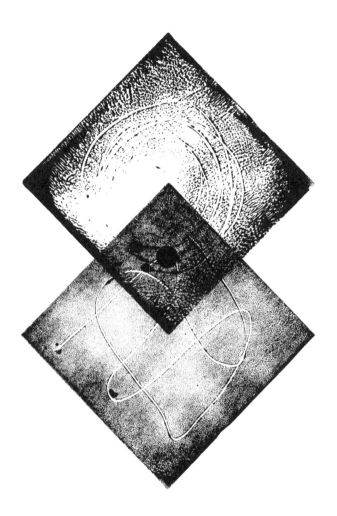

If you play,
You know there's a game.
If there's a game,
You know you can figure it out.

The secret to greatness?
Hard work and persistence.
The secret to happiness?
Loving the process.
The secret to fun?
Play.
The secret to these secrets?
Stop thinking, start doing.

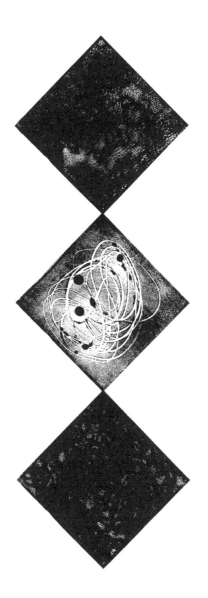

Own your uniqueness.
Cancel the noise that tells you
To conform to "the norm."
Trust yourself,
Listen to what you know is your truth.
Go for it: Be you! Do you!

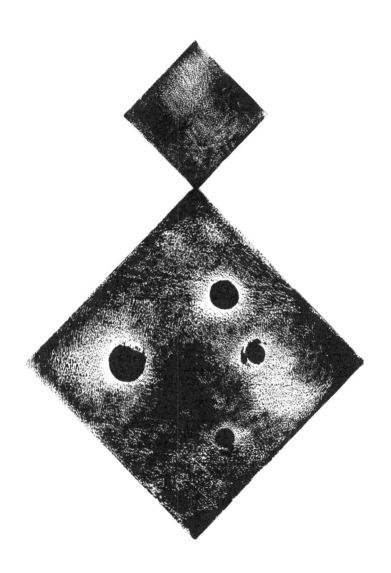

The more you get how you're affecting others (and life),
The more you raise yourself to higher standards.

Because at a higher level, you are them, and they are you
—and *together*—you are co-creating reality.

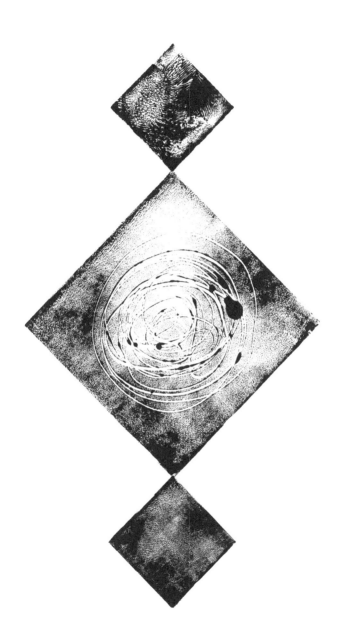

You can add a little bit of vibrancy
To your voice,
You can add a little bit of flair
To the way you dress,
You can add a little bit of grace
To your movements,
You can add a little bit of beauty
To your environment.
Why?
Just because *you can.*

Rise above your thoughts,
As if you were in a tower,
And observe them like passing clouds.

Now, who could ever judge passing clouds?

Life rewards you when you work hard.
Life listens when you tell the truth.
Life loves you when you play.

You don't need to call yourself spiritual
To align your actions with your True Self.
You don't need to call yourself an artist
To create art every single day.
You don't need to call yourself a lover
To love deeply.

It's never *what* you call yourself.
It's *how* you show up in life.

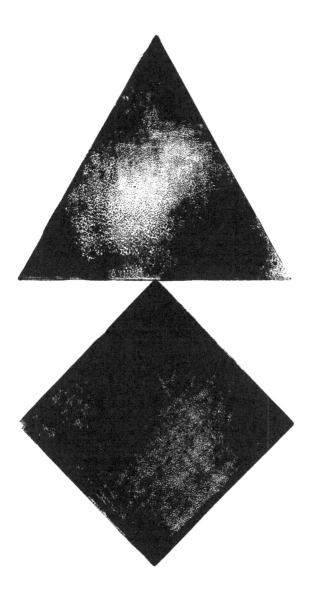

In times of joy,
Shine on.
In times of darkness,
Shine on.
You are here to shine,
So let your light out!
What else would you be here for?

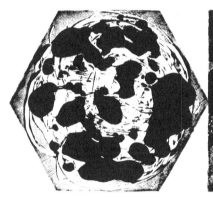

If your life is like the ocean,
Spitting out thundering waves,
Pick up a board and start surfing.

You would never attack a storm
With a hatchet.
Stop trying to outthink your problems.

The freedom you seek is in the presence
Of your ground of being.

You are much more powerful
Than you think.
Now, trust your power.

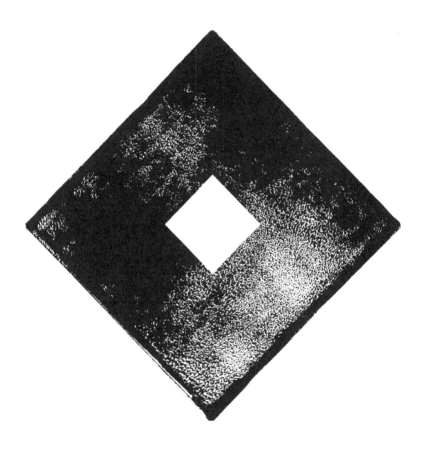

Create a game of life
That works for you.
Learn from it.
Grow from it.
Love the process.
Try again.
That's how you win.

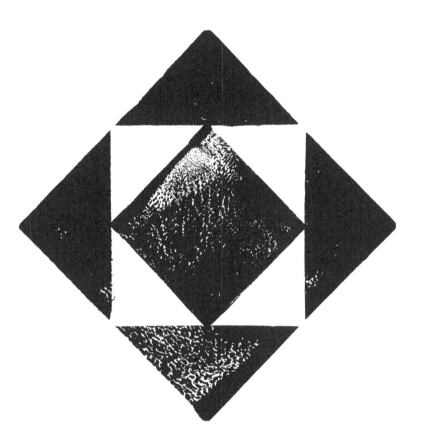

Don't mistake your state of mind
For your reality.

Engage fully with whatever
Is in front of you.

Let go!
Let's go!

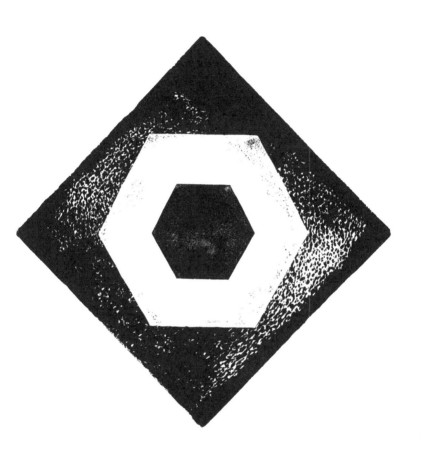

You will never find light
By following darkness.
Let your light guide you to the light.

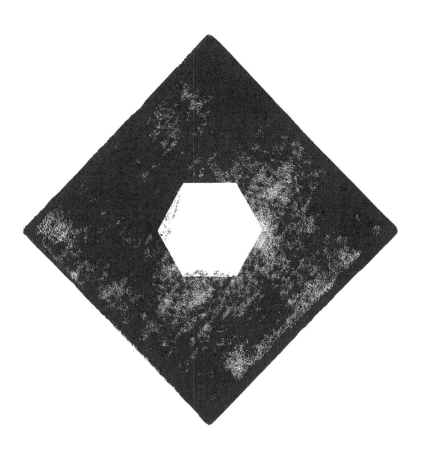

Ask yourself daily:
"Am I contracting?"
Or
"Am I expanding?"

Your answer will create your destiny.

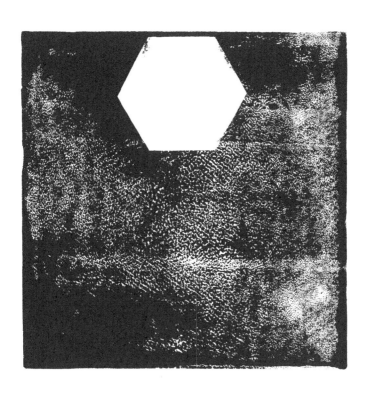

Connect with your True Self
To find the answer.
Go from ME to WE.
Aren't we all living together
In this reality?

A wish is formless,
Until you start the journey.
You are formless,
Until you unfold into life.

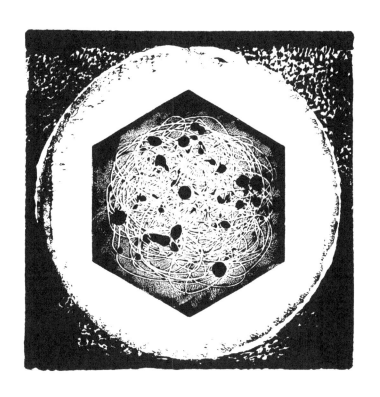

Don't trust your mind
To manage your soul.

Meet two robbers:
Fear from the past
And anxiety about the future.

Kick these robbers out of your life
By centering yourself in the present.

Now, everything is possible.

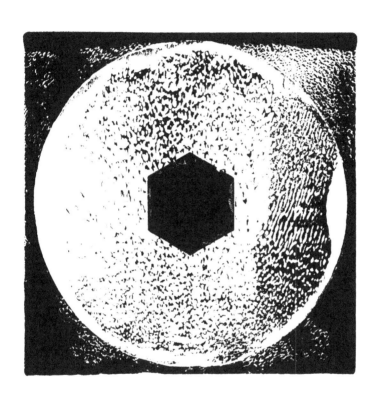

Buy your escape in virtual reality,
Or
Infuse the present with your spiritual vitality.
The choice is yours.

There's a secret temple within you
Where a light shines radiant.

Infinitely bright,
Centered in everything.

Don't be a stranger.
Be still.
This is your ticket in.

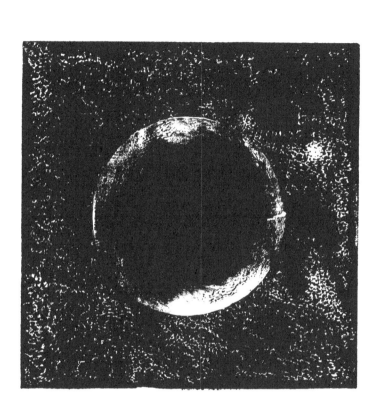

Stop running after what's out there:
You are what you seek.

Look inside.
You're *it*.

Let yourself be your everything
In the state of your everythingness.

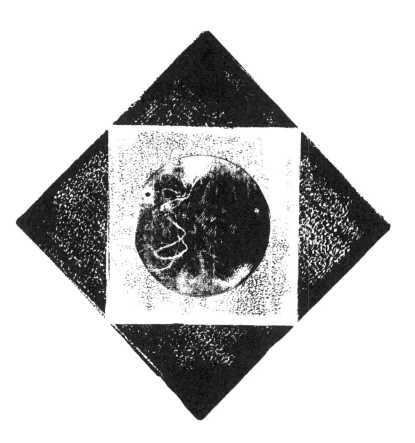

I have faith in you,
Because you are on a quest,

Exploring,
Creating,
Loving,
Shining.

I have faith in you,
Because you are living your truth.

Meditate.
Mediate.
Transcend.
The trance ends.

ON

SHINING

Joanne Abellera: *In the book, what do you mean by "shine"?*

Guillaume Wolf: The shine is the expression of your spirit into the world. It's the brilliance of your soul's signature.

JA: *Here, you're introducing the idea of a game, and play.*

GW: Yes, it's because when you look into the human spirit, the sense of play comes along.

JA: *How?*

GW: On the one hand, a human life is a very serious affair. But on the other hand, a human soul has a certain playfulness, a lightness to it. This is why the word "enthusiasm" comes from the Greek *enthousiasmos* which means "divine inspiration."

JA: *At some point you speak about flair, grace, and beauty. How do they relate to the soul?*

GW: Well, let's look at beauty. Let's imagine a dancer, dancing. On a purely practical level, you could say that dance doesn't create anything concrete. Intellectually, it's not something you could easily describe as being "productive." Yet, dance is so powerful because it operates on an entirely different level. It's a celebration of the soul. The dancer feels it, and the viewer feels it too. It's a sense of play that comes from the soul to feed the soul. And this food for the soul is something we need today, more than ever.

JA: *Can you expand on the sense of play?*

GW: When you play, you enter into a relationship with life where your imagination reshuffles reality. This is the classic suspension of disbelief that's part of every story. It always starts with this question: *What if?* Now, tell me why do we love stories so much?

JA: *. . . Because we need them.*

GW: Yes! Again, this is food for the soul. There's no better way to put it. You need stories to feed your soul, and you need play in your life to connect with these stories.

JA: *So how do you shine?*

GW: By letting your soul speak. Art is a great vehicle for that. Service is another amazing way. Love is another path. Whatever this is for you, it's the idea of doing something to fill your heart with joy; not because it's a logical choice, or because you think it's going to make you money.

JA: *You write: "Create a game of life that works for you." How do you do that?*

GW: By organizing your life so that it nurtures your soul. This is the highest game there is. And this is the hardest too. But it's far from impossible; actually, if we're committed, we can all do it.

JA: *How so?*

GW: First, I'm going to make a blunt statement. I'm going to start by saying that most of us are going through life half-asleep. So the first thing is to wake up and ask: "Have I been living my life at my full potential?" And it's a tough question because . . .

JA: *Most of us haven't.*

GW: That's right. So you start with this realization—you wake up. And it can be tough at first. Next, you use your imagination and say: "*If* I were to act at my full potential starting today, how would I take care of my relationships, my work, my health, my art, and my spiritual life?" And here you simply imagine this upgraded version of yourself and all the things you would start doing differently. And the funny thing here, is that you already know exactly what to do.

JA: *I can see that.*

GW: And the final step is the most important: You bring in the sense of play and start acting on your vision. You bring in your presence to everything you do, just for the fun of it. You shine, because you want to have fun playing. Here, there's no pressure to succeed; there's no "doing it wrong." You start acting at your full potential just to see what it would be like. You wake up an hour earlier and surprise your partner with breakfast. You create a new project. You start exercising. You eat better.

You read inspiring work. This is a process of connection supported by a celebration of your soul. If you allow yourself to play, there's almost no limit on how much you can grow.

JA: *Can we all do that?*

GW: Of course we can. I see it with my students all the time. If you create this space for possibility and play, it's just fun trying new things out. And if you're not doing it; it's simply because you think you can't. That's the core reason. But what are the alternatives? What else would you be doing with your life to find happiness?

JA: *You write: "Buy your escape in virtual reality; or, infuse the present with your spiritual vitality."*

Gw: Exactly! And the choice is yours.

Don't skip a beat.
Wake your world up.

Collect them all!

"GET INVOLVED!"

Hello, friend,

I hope you've enjoyed exploring this book and that it will inspire you to go out there and do great things.

This book and its companions are an experiment in publishing: It's a labor of love.

So if you really like this book and want to see more in the future, *get involved!* Please join me in this adventure by supporting it.

What you can do:
Please post about this book on your social media platform:
Use **#YouAreAQuest**
and you can also tag me on

Instagram **@profG.co**
TikTok **@profG.co**

Please leave a review on **Amazon.com** and share your story about how this book is a part of your life. It really helps, and it's super-nice to hear from you.

I really appreciate your support.

Guillaume "Prof. G"

GO DEEPER: FREE VIDEO COURSE

Inspired? What's next?

This book is an invitation to reflect and explore, to open the doors of your imagination. But there's more . . .

You are invited to take an online course with Guillaume Wolf "Prof. G" to go deeper.

Simply visit: **www.profg.co/free**
to sign up and access the course.

ABOUT THE AUTHOR

Author, teacher, and spirituality explorer Guillaume Wolf "Prof. G" helps you dream big dreams, and make them real.

Through his books and online courses, Prof. G's mission is to empower, inspire, and challenge creatives of all walks of life to use their creative skills to bring meaningful change in their lives and make a positive impact in the world.

Prof. G is an associate professor at ArtCenter College of Design in Pasadena, California, where he teaches communication design and the psychology of change.

www.ProfG.co

Made in the USA
Las Vegas, NV
11 December 2021

37183751R00163